In-Person Cold Calling

15 Steps To Attaining Multi-Million Dollar Corporate Clients.

Most people are afraid of Cold Calling. Some of the reasons can be lack of confidence, fear of rejection or fear of failure. It can also test your mental toughness and work ethic.

In this revolutionary Itty Bitty Book, Anthony Camacho, International Best Selling Author, shares some of the best secrets that he has garnered over the past 20 years, to help you secure corporate clients and seven figures in sales. Through this book, you will build the confidence and techniques needed to grow your business and your revenue stream.

- If prospects don't know you exist how can you ever be an option to do business with them.
- People need to know your name whether they do business with you or not. COLD CALL the WORLD and make it warm.

If you want to start growing your business immediately, pick up a copy of this powerful little book today

Your Amazing Itty Bitty®
Little Black Book of Successful In-Person Cold Calling

The HITMAN'S 15 Steps To Close Multi-Million Dollar Corporate Clients

Anthony Camacho
BEST SELLING AUTHOR

Published by Itty Bitty® Publishing
A subsidiary of S & P Productions, Inc.

Printed in the United States of America

Itty Bitty Publishing
311 Main Street, Suite D
El Segundo, CA 90245
(310) 640-8885

ISBN: 978-1-950326-38-9

*To my partner in life, love & adventure -
Tanya - thank you for being my inspiration,
best friend and fellow extreme sports lover.
You bring so much joy, peace and fulfillment
to my life. You truly are my lighthouse. I look
forward to more business and travel
adventures together - love Anthony.*

Stop by our Itty Bitty® website to find
interesting information about sales

www.IttyBittyPublishing.com

Or visit Anthony at
www.anthonycamacho.com

Or email Anthony at
hitman@camachocoaching.com

Table of Contents

Introduction

Introduction

They call me the Hitman, because *"Hitmen don't make appointments"*. And that's exactly what I want you to do – to turn up at a key place of business unannounced, in-person, to land and secure lucrative deals, endless referrals and even make a few friends.

What I'm going to share with you is the lost - but very much alive - art of cold calling. I've distilled more than 20 years' experience from cold-calling the most unpalatable of products – selling funeral plots door-to-door for the Catholic Church – to the most glamorous – securing Fortune 100 clients with one handshake and without one appointment.

Now celebrating the completion of over 700 paid national and international multi-day workshops and seminars, I hope to give you a strong and successful foundation to get out there, to be more and to sell more. Because when implemented, this book will not only help you overcome your fear of rejection but it will also help you build your confidence, your sales skills and your results.

Step 1
Destroy Hesitation

Congratulations on adding cold calling to your sales tool arsenal! Cold calling really is a great way to create new leads and secure new clients, but it's also not for the faint hearted. In fact, the idea of cold calling a few powerful players may seem like a great idea sitting at your desk but in practice it may trigger some self-doubt – which is natural. Implement the game plan below and turn those feelings of nerves and fear into excitement!

1. Do your research, know where you're headed and who you're asking for – you want the decision maker.
2. Get out of ego. Meditate. Leave behind all fear, worry, doubt and uncertainty.
3. Walk into the place of business and get comfortable with the surroundings.
4. Your focus is to get face-to-face with the person you want to sell to but first, you have to find out who that is.

Steps to destroy hesitation

- Look for an employee to build on what you already know:
  - Who is the decision maker?
  - What is his or her name?
  - Are they in today?
  - Where is their office?
- Go to the reception desk and announce that you are there to see the decision maker. Be confident and authoritative, present like the decision maker is expecting you – even though they're not!
- Your focus is to be visible in the marketplace – you want your name to be buzzing around their business; be memorable for the right reasons.
- Forget about perfect execution: life is not scripted and neither is in-person cold calling. Perfection doesn't exist.
- Know that this is not your last visit, at the very least; you will come away with valuable information for next time.
- In life and in sales, the one who hesitates and second-guesses is the one who loses.

Step 2
Sell Yourself First

Most sales are lost in the mind. If you can't sell yourself, don't expect to sell anyone else. Before you start your cold calls visualize the entire exchange play out in your head. It is only impossible if you say it is impossible.

1. Set a time every morning to visualize the successful cold calling experience.
2. Make sure you're in a comfortable place with no distractions.
3. Focus your mind on only the visualization – avoid thinking of other tasks.
4. See yourself happily walking into the business, getting straight to the decision makers and exchanging handshakes as well as the beginning of the entire sales process.
5. Visualize the closing of the deal and the excitement that it brings.

More steps to sell yourself first

- In your mind's eye it's not enough to see it you must feel it too.
- Let your mind take you through the emotion and experience as though it has already happened.
- Replaying this positive exchange over and over again, helps remove unnecessary worry, doubt and hesitation.
- Top athletes and executives use this meditative visual rehearsal to help achieve and exceed their goals.
- Create the new reality from the inside out.

Step 3
In-Person Cold Calling Is Not Dead

A lot of people say that cold calling is dead and not necessary to close deals. The truth is that those who say this would rather hide behind a telephone, email blast or social media direct message spamming. The truth is, the myth – that cold calling is dead – serves such critics because they are often too afraid to cold call, don't know how to cold call or just don't want to do the work.

1. Cold calling builds relationships faster than impersonal emails, phone calls and social media reach outs.
2. Cold calling makes you more memorable.
3. Cold calling creates 'mental market share', particularly if you leave a small gift as a signature calling card.
4. Having a live interaction to introduce yourself is more powerful than an email or phone call.

More in-person cold calling is not dead

- You get more face time in person, and as a result, more time to ask for referrals.
- You can read the body language and facial expressions of your prospect – a huge advantage for adjusting your pitch.
- You might not be able to reach as many people in person cold calling, versus email blasts, but your 'opt-in' rate and conversions will be much higher.
- Fortune always favors the bold and cold calling is all about being bold!

Step 4
Let Go Of Attachments

Be unattached to the outcome, as though you are a third party observer. Remove all ego from the process and be as detached from a 'yes' as much as you are detached from a 'no'. This is a process and forming any kind of an attachment – positive or negative – is kryptonite and will undermine your state of mind and therefore your success.

1. It's not about instant gratification.
2. It's not about you: it's about the message that you're bringing to the world.
3. Some will hear it, some will not.
4. Those that you are meant to serve will hear it, remember: 'You can't say the wrong thing to the right person, or the right thing to the wrong person'.
5. Those that say no, at the very least, may become new referrals or even friends.

More Letting Go Of Attachments

When most people cold call they have an investment or attachment to the result. If you mark every element of the cold call as a success, then the cold call itself becomes fun and rewarding. If you make the cold call just about the sale, not only will you miss the fun but, you'll probably miss the sale as well.

So remember...

- Just getting to shake a person's hand is a success.
- Just getting to say your name and your business is a success.
- Just getting to share about your business is a success.
- Walking into a new door, at a new place of business, is a success.
- Getting to the decision maker or influencer is a success.

Step 5
Love the Hunt

You must absolutely love what you do and be passionate and tenacious about cold calling. Just like a musician spends hours and hours honing their craft, you must too. What tools do you need to practice in the world of sales and cold calling? Is it introducing yourself to new prospects? Is it 'fact finding' about their business? Is it your ability to uncover who the decision maker is, so you know who to target? Give yourself permission to learn, hone and 'perfect' your tools and know that knowledge and deals often come from the lessons learned. Cold calling comes from inspiration, not desperation, so cold call for the love of sales and go enjoy the hunt.

1. Love what you sell.
2. Know what your commission is from every product.
3. Know what products are available to sell.
4. Believe that your product is a game changer.
5. Sell solutions not just products.

More About loving the hunt

The mindset of professional sales people, who outwit, outlast and outplay the competition is part of sales mastery.

- Genuinely believe that your product is the best choice for your customer.
- Believe that what you are doing is part of your purpose.
- Know that you are changing the world, one cold call at a time.
- Every cold call is a good use of your time, regardless of its outcome.
- Put a 100 percent into your day, so no matter what the outcome you feel fulfilled.

Step 6
Dress Like A Boss

When cold calling, you want to avoid giving anyone an excuse to think you don't belong there; and so it is imperative to show up looking like the polished professional you are. Dress like the person you are going to meet - an executive, a decision maker, a boss.

1. Wear a clean and pressed suit, shirt and tie; or for the ladies a skirt suit and heels.
2. Make sure your shoes are clean and shined.
3. Be color coordinated.
4. Align your buttons, fix your tie, collar or jacket and make sure your clothes are not stained or ripped.
5. Be clean-shaven.
6. Have a clean and neat hairstyle.
7. Make sure that your nails and hands are clean.
8. Make sure that your breath smells good.
9. Double-check your teeth, nose and ears.
10. Smell freshly showered and good.

More about dressing like a boss

You don't have to go out and buy the most expensive clothing. Make sure what you wear fits well and looks good.

- Buy dark interchangeable suits:
  - Charcoal gray
  - Black
  - Dark blue
- Solid button down shirts:
  - Blue
  - White
  - French cuffs if possible
- Invest in a pair of stylish, laced brown and black shoes with matching belts.
- Buy some versatile, solid ties in red, yellow and blue.

Check your appearance in a nearby bathroom before making your introductions.

Step 7
Closing Ratios

Your closing ratio is defined as the number of 'calls' it takes to get one appointment, one meeting or just one sale. And when you understand your closing ratio, you can easily calculate through simple math just how many 'leads' you need to lock in one sale; and then how many leads are needed to meet weekly, monthly and quarterly sales targets. From these figures a sales professional can very easily forecast the number of 'calls' needed to generate a desired income. And, because every salesperson's closing ratio is different, it's crucial that you know yours.

1. What is your closing ratio when you in-person cold call?
2. How many doors do you need to walk into each day / week / month to lock in one appointment?
3. How many follow-up 'touch points' do you need on the phone or in person to secure an appointment?
4. How many appointments do you need to close one sale?

More about closing ratios

- Make a log and journal details.
- Track how many appointments are needed each day / week / month to close one deal.
- Discover your personal sales formula: What is the average length of time before you close a deal? What is the average value of one deal?
- Be aware that 80% of all deals are closed on the 12th contact.

Step 8
Days & Times To Hunt

Like many things in life, timing is everything and cold calling is no different. Not only are there certain days of the week to be avoided when turning up unannounced, but also certain times of the day. Over the past 20 years, I've found the following times to minimize and maximize my cold calling.

1. Avoid Mondays. In general, most decision makers are in meetings, prepping for the week ahead.
2. Fridays are not the best either. Many organizations have sales meetings on Friday mornings. They will be reviewing the past week as well as prepping and rallying the troops for bumper weekend business. Many have also mentally 'checked out'.
3. Avoid the last two days of the month as they are trying to close last minute deals to crush sales quotas.
4. Rainy days are the best days to go out and cold call, because most competitors stay home; as do most customers.

More about days and times to hunt

- Tuesday, Wednesday and Thursday are great days to cold call.
- The best time to cold call on Tuesdays, Wednesdays and Thursdays is between 9:30am - 11:45am.
- Specifically, 9:30am is great because it allows the decision makers to settle in for the day.
- While 11:45am is also fantastic because it's just before lunch, you can still catch the decision maker or even offer to take them to lunch!
- The next best times for in-person cold calling is between 1:15pm to 4:45pm, but beware of the post-lunch energy slump and the home time hurry shuffle!

In the past I have also broken all these time frames and days and just trusted my gut instinct to walk in anyway. Use these time frames as a guide, not as an excuse to wait until another day!

Step 9
Cold Calling Your 'Hot Zone'

You have to be realistic – there are only so many hours in a day and so many places you can physically get to in one day. Driving, or windshield time, is dead time. You want to create a geographical 'hot zone' that will maximize your cold calling time and your earning potential. In this day and age, where everyone sends emails and makes phone calls, what will set you apart is that personal touch; which will also leave a strong impression on your prospect and the decision makers themselves.

1. Identify where a 'cluster' of your potential clients exist.
2. Draw a radius around this 'hot zone' and dedicate an entire day to the area.
3. Create a daily cold calling route.
4. Try to see the same prospects on the same days to create familiarity.

More about cold calling your 'Hot Zone'

- Start furthest away from your home and work backwards, cold calling along the way – much like a newspaper delivery boy in days gone by.
- Map out drive times and shortcuts.
- Make sure you have plenty of snacks and drinks for the road, including chewing gum.
- Even when running personal errands, take advantage of every opportunity and scout prospects in the area.

Step 10
Create Mental Market Share

Always ask yourself, *'What can I do to leave a positive impression? How can I stand out?'* You want to get to the point where you start to create space in a person's head, where certain things remind them of you – in other words, mental market share.

1. Make routine visits on the same days, preferably at the same time.
2. Create an expectation in the prospect's head that they are going to see you to the point where they will 'miss you' if you don't show up.
3. Make a log of each visit, including date, time and brief notes of the conversation and any actions to take.
4. Brand yourself and create a signature look to stand out from your competitors and be memorable, e.g. be the 'pink tie guy'.

More about creating Mental Market Share

- Understand who you are prospecting and what they like.
- Occupy space in their head to think of you with positive pleasant reminders.
- Remember personal details and current events such as vacations, family members and achievements.
- Leave a little gift behind that they will appreciate.

Step 11
The Power of Internal Influencers

While it is crucial to identify decision makers on your cold calls, it is also equally important to get to know the different players within the organization. You want to create as many allies and friends as you can so that your name becomes a positive buzzword. Creating friends and allies also provides you with a slew of information about the business' operations, current competitors, internal alliances and current affairs that can provide further opportunities to close more deals.

1. Influencers are close to decision makers and are trusted advisors or even friends.
2. Influencers can provide you with great insight to prep you for a proposal, presentation and even help close a deal without you having to apply too much pressure on the decision maker.
3. Connect with influencers on social media and comment supportively on their posts.
4. Get insight about the culture and environment from the influencers.
5. Get insight about the competitors from the influencers.

More about the power of internal influencers

- Be approachable and likable with everyone.
- Treat everyone with equal and great importance – from the janitor to the CEO.
- Keep a log of all your interactions and discoveries.
- Find out what community programs they are involved in and if possible, become a supporter and/or sponsor as well.
- Discover how you can be an advocate for their business.

Step 12
Closing Appointments

Put a dollar sign next to every appointment in your planner because every meeting is potentially another deal closed. As a result, it is crucial you continually make, set and close new appointments on a daily basis.

1. In the first appointment don't be overly concerned with closing the deal.
2. The main objective to closing deals is to focus on getting the appointment - appointments come first, sales follow.
3. Be genuine, be more concerned with understanding the wants and needs of the business than closing the deal.
4. Listen and align the right product or program to close the deal.

More about closing appointments

- Come up with creative ways to set appointments, e.g. offer a free training or service for staff.
- Appointments give you more face time with the prospect.
- 'Face time' makes you more likeable, more familiar and more trustworthy.
- It's harder for a decision maker to say *'no'* when they know, like and trust you AND you're sitting opposite them.

Step 13
Friendships = Long-Term Sales

Adopt a positive mindset and you will see that your cold calling route will turn into a social occasion that brings constant wins.

Because with cold calling ...

1. You can secure multiple sales opportunities.
2. You can make powerful allies and supporters.
3. Even if you miss the sale you could still create a new friendship.
4. When circumstances change within the company and they're open to doing business – you're likely to get the first call.
5. When the decision maker hires you and then moves to another location they will bring your business and services along.

More On Friendships = Long-Term Sales

There are many opportunities for creating long lasting friendships and ongoing business with cold calling, even when the answer is 'no'.

- Forming friendships gives valuable insight on competitors and other vendors.
- Future opportunities may still arise, so touch base and always circle back.
- Always ask for referrals - when people say 'no' as they often feel bad about it and actively want to help another way.
- Look for the long play, the bigger picture beyond the next sale.
- You can secure thousands of dollars with friendships in business.

Step 14
How & Why To Ask For Referrals

Most sales people – as well as business owners – fail to consistently ask for referrals either because they forget or don't like to ask for them. But if you fail to ask for referrals you are literally leaving tens of thousands of dollars on the table. The only shots in life you miss are the ones you don't take.

1. A referral is not a reference. A referral is asking people you do business with who else they know that can use your services.
2. Use the 5:1 ratio: ask for five referrals up front. If they don't have five, ask for three. If they don't have three, ask for one. At the very least you'll get one.
3. You can ask anyone for a referral – you don't even need to have done business with them.
4. Referrals are new leads for free.

More about referrals

- Referrals can put life back into a cold sales funnel / pipeline.
- Use your friends as practice, ask them for referrals.
- Write down the names of your top 10 raving fans and ask them each for five referrals.
- Sales professionals leave thousands of dollars on the table by not making referrals part of their day-to-day sales goals.

Step 15
Resilience Pays

In order to have continued success in cold calling you really do need to have the ability to keep knocking on doors whether you feel like it or not. And it doesn't matter if it's hot outside, or raining, if it's fun or if it's a drag, cold calling is an opportunity; because you never know what door you'll walk into, what hand you will shake and how that one exchange will change your life.

1. It's not a feeling it's a choice.
2. It takes perseverance.
3. Be your own cheer squad – encourage yourself.
4. Maintain momentum and energy levels. Rest and recover to overcome fatigue.
5. Rejection is part of the process: fear is excitement without breath; so breathe and get excited!
6. Keep going until you get an appointment – shake more hands!

More about how resilience pays

Cold calling can make you millions in sales. Just one handshake can secure international deals. Just one door – when opened – can change your life. There are a million mental barriers as to why you shouldn't cold call, give into them and you've lost.

- Cold calling will stretch you.
- Cold calling will make you grow.
- Cold calling will challenge you.
- Cold calling will increase your ability to be courageous and bold.
- Cold calling can change your life with just one handshake.
- Cold calling is for the ambitious.
- Cold calling is for those who won't settle.
- Cold calling is for sales warriors.

You've finished. Before you go...

Tweet/share that you finished this book.

Please star rate this book.

Reviews are solid gold to writers. Please take a few minutes to give us some itty bitty feedback.

ABOUT THE AUTHOR

In sales circles he's known as the Hitman. A nickname earned not from the gang life he escaped as a teen; but for his ability to turn 'cold into sold'.

Having worked with start-ups to $40 million 'small businesses' Anthony Camacho is a sales and performance mentor to everyday entrepreneurs as well as Fortune 100/500 companies.

A multi-published best-selling author, Anthony has cold called millions of dollars in sales and has been so successful in his industry that he became the youngest regional sales manager for a large multinational consulting corporation.

A former Dale Carnegie Coach and certified sales coach through the Institute for Professional Excellence in Coaching, Anthony has 20 years of experience in cold calling, generating new prospects, bringing in new business, closing deals and managing sales teams.

Working with corporate clients, executives, business rockstars and entrepreneurs. He is the CEO and creator of the Sales Performance Training Company The Top Producer Factory.

If you enjoyed this book you might also benefit from the Itty Bitty® Books found on our www.IttyBittyPublishing.com website or other digital sites.